DARE TO LIVE YOUR BEST LIFE NOW

50 Simple Truths To Discover Your Passion & Live A Life You Love

by Angel I. Erediauwa

TABLE OF CONTENT

45. CONFIDENCE, THE NEW SEXY

46. GO ON, LIVE, LOVE & LAUGH

47. STOP WORRYING SO MUCH

48. BROADEN YOUR LIFE

49. LIVE OUT LOUD

50. DO SOMETHING NICE FOR SOMEONE ELSE/GIVE BACK

INTRODUCTION

Hi and thank you for getting my book, I hope it inspires you to take the action to live the life that you love.

Do you want to wake up with purpose everyday because you are living the life that you love, do you want to take action today to start creating and enjoying your ideal life?

Sometimes, We all fall into the trap of feeling insecure and need to overcome some of our false beliefs; we get into a rut and feel stuck and need the confidence and boldness to live life on our own terms. And sometimes, we need those truths that will remind us to be happy today.

Taking action does not always mean changing direction or location, it also means doing the best with what you have right now towards creating the life you want. It means becoming the person you want to be and the person that attracts what you want.

For those times when you need a boost of motivation or a kick in your behind or when you just need to feel good about yourself, this is a book you can have with you always and refer to again and again that gives you simple truths to remind you to stay positive and in a good mind frame. These truths will dare you to live your best life now.

FORGET THE COMPLICATED WAY OF LIVING

Life happens and can be complicated but most times, we make it even more complicated, don't get bogged down and overwhelmed by the complexities of life, instead of focusing on what could go wrong, start focusing on what you want things to be like, this in turn will change your perspective about life. Life begins to get confusing and complicated when we start losing faith in ourselves, when you don't believe in yourself, it rubs you of your confidence to live a less complicated life.

Focus on what makes you happy and let go of things that make you doubt yourself. Don't hold on to what you cannot control, accept that there are some things that are beyond your control, then let them go. Sometimes, you have to let go of the good to get the best.

"LIFE'S COMPLICATED ENOUGH, DON'T MAKE IT EVEN MORE DIFFICULT"

Spend more time with the right people, this is quite easy really, just limit your time with people who don't make you feel good about yourself, and spend more time with people who make you happy and inspire you to be your best. Trust yourself, this is one thing people often forget to do, recall the times you had made good decisions and felt good about yourself, write down these times and replay them in your mind and begin to trust yourself again.

DON'T SWEAT THE SMALL STUFF

Small stuff happens all the time, it's part of life, however, don't allow it take over your life and take away the colour from your life. Often we allow ourselves get too worked up about things that are insignificant; we make mountains out of a molehill. Some people make a big deal out of the littlest things, if they burnt the toast, it's spoils their whole morning, if they make a mistake at work, it's like the world's unhappy with them. Don't beat yourself up over the little problems of life, get the right perspective and deal with it head on.

Often times, people let these small concerns and problems pile up, they get worked up over each till it stacks up and they are walking around like a ticking time bomb. Let go of the small nagging issues, some things are just not worth your time after all. I heard a story about a couple in a restaurant, the woman received a phone call and said so dramatically 'Oh no, Oh my God, that is just terrible to hear, what are we going to do?' Her husband thought for sure she had received some bad news and he asked her what the matter was, she held the phone away from her and said to her husband 'They've run out of chocolate cookies in the store'.

There are many of these little problems that occur every day in our lives, don't let them take over your life, don't dwell so much on them that you miss enjoying your life.

Focus on getting the right things done, gear your energy towards tasks that are more important to you and that are most effective.

WHAT ARE YOU MAKING 'IT' MEAN?

We are humans and we attach meaning to events. THAT is what we do. I learned a very valuable lesson recently and it was this. Life is meaningless, things happen but we are the ones who create meaning to what has happened. We attach different meanings to life's occurrences. And often times, we assign negative intent to things that happen and to other people's innocent actions.

This has been a very powerful lesson for me. It means that I am really in control of what I make my life mean and the great news is that I can make it mean what I want to make it mean.

For example, say your spouse leaves an item of clothing on the floor, you can attach a whole bunch of meaning to this, it could mean your spouse is too tired because they have been working too hard, or they are not feeling too well, or you could make it mean that your spouse is taking you for granted, or doesn't appreciate you etc., and get this, whatever meaning you attach to this event (your spouse leaving their clothing on the floor) will have a significant impact on the rest of your day.

Don't default to attaching a negative meaning to events or to other people's actions, this will usually have a negative impact on your day and your life. You have a set reality and meaning of Life and this is responsible for where you are today, how you feel and what you think, to start creating a new reality, you have to change your meaning of life.

> "LIFE HAS NOTHING AGAINST YOU, LIFE DOES NOT HOLD A GRUDGE AGAINST YOU, LIFE HAPPENS, DON'T LIVE LIKE THE WORLD IS AGAINST YOU"

FORGET OTHER PEOPLE'S OPINIONS

We live too much based on other people's opinions of us; don't be enslaved by other people's opinions. We all have the desire to be loved and liked by people; the truth is that even if you are the very best person in the world, some people will hate that about you. More over, do you really want to give such power over your life to others? Opinions are a dime a dozen and they come just as quickly. One of the greatest freedoms is living life free of what everyone else thinks of you. Don't get your mind so cluttered with the opinion of others that you can't even hear yourself. Don't lose yourself in other people's opinions,

'Don't let the opinion of others become your reality' – Les Brown
'Most people are other people. Their thoughts are someone else's opinions, their lives a mimicry, their passions a quotation'- Oscar Wilde

What does it take for you to be happy, and why would you sacrifice this happiness for others, the truth is that some people are frustrated with their own lives and yet you would sacrifice your happiness because of these people's opinions.

A lesson you ought to learn is that everyone else is too busy dealing with his or her own lives to make you feel better about yours.

Follow the course that is yours, it does not matter what people say, one thing is certain, and that is the life you envision for yourself is far beyond what others can imagine and you are the best person for the job.

THE NECESSARY ASSUMPTION THEORY

We are built to thrive and bloom in a positive and loving environment, you may have heard it said that love is the greatest force, it is not a cliché, it is a fact. When everything is good with you, everything is good with the world, because you see the world through your perceptions and your thoughts.

Have you met people who can't even say something nice about themselves? When people look at them, they become self-conscious and their first thought is that there is something wrong with them, now listen, there is something I call the necessary assumption.

This theory states that you are amazing, powerful, intelligent, lovely, and attractive and all that is wonderful and good and you have to know it and learn to own it. It states that you expect people around you to notice you for your awesomeness.

"WHEN EVERYTHING IS RIGHT WITH YOU, DON'T THINK THE UNIVERSE IS OUT OF BALANCE, EXPECT GREAT THINGS TO HAPPEN TO YOU, THEY ARE NOT TOO GOOD TO BE TRUE, THEY ARE HAPPENING TO THE RIGHT PERSON, YOU!"

It is funny how the wrong things stand out to us first in any situation, that is the reason why people can make statements like this is too good to be true, or why people always expect something bad to happen to them, you complement someone on their appearance and instead of saying thank you, they look for something to criticise about themselves, because it makes them feel better to have something negative about themselves, so as not to upset the balance of the universe.

Experience the wonder of you and the beauty of you. Experience your essence. Experience the miracle that is you.

FIND YOUR HAPPINESS IN WHERE YOU ARE

It does not matter where you are today, find your happiness in where you are, have the mind-set that you may not be where you want to be today but at least, you are another day closer, you are not where you were yesterday because believe it or not, you are growing and developing everyday. Every decision, choice you make, every perception you form, every information you receive, the actions you take, the books you read, the people you meet, challenges you face and many more factors, determine and shape who you are, some are factors you may control and others are factors beyond your control but all these shape who you are. The question is, are you becoming whom you like or are you becoming whom you don't like?

A word of advice, since you are developing and growing anyway, you might as well put in the effort to develop into that person you want to be. You don't stop growing or becoming who you are just because you decide not to do anything about it, life doesn't stop just because you fold your arms, it is up to you to take the circumstances, the information and these factors and turn them to your advantage.

So think of all the great things about you today and speak them out loud. One of my favourite quotes that inspire me greatly is by Jo Blackwell-Preston and it says

"Don't you dare, for one more second, surround yourself with people who are not aware of the greatness that you are."

STOP COMPLAINING, BUT IF YOU WANT TO, COMPLAIN ABOUT THE RIGHT THINGS

Someone gave me an advice that I am sure you will find helpful, she said, even when you are upset and frustrated and you want to grumble and complain, go ahead, but just ensure you are complaining about every good thing about you, complain about the great things happening to you, complain about the good things you have in your life right now. This may be funny but it sure works because even in this state, you are focused on the important things and before you know it, you will complain your way back up to being happy and grateful again.

This may come as a surprise to you, or not, life is full of challenges and difficulties and this is because we have to relate with different elements and factors, man is complex being, with different views, opinions, beliefs and emotions, get a few people to live together for a while and you will encounter on a smaller scale what we experience on a world scale everyday, egos and opinions clashing, perceptions formed, prejudice and judgements etc.

So do not blame the challenges that you come against, they come with the structure and make up of the world, but the great news is that you have the ability to control your own world.

THE APPROVAL SYNDROME

"No one but you knows how hard you work, how many hours you put in behind the scenes, so rely on yourself for approval, not the outside world".

Of course it is great when others appreciate your work and recognise who you are and what you do, but your joy should not come completely from that.

Your ideas and choices don't have to be on everyone's approval list, as long as they are the best choices for you and are not harmful to others. At the end of the day, you are the one who is going to live with those choices and they should make you proud.

It is natural for you to want other people to like you and to approve of you, but don't let that become a burden, a self imposed necessity that designs your behaviour and actions to constantly reassure you of other people's approval.

CELEBRATE EVEN THE SMALLEST OF SUCCESSES

You are the only one who knows the victories you have won, no matter how insignificant they may seem so celebrate them anyway. It may be a small step you have taken towards your goal, celebrate that step, don't look at what you should have done that you didn't do, celebrate what you have done instead because that would encourage you to do even more.

For example, you have always wanted to start your business or something as simple as wanting to learn a new skill, you have talked about it for years and every January, you have said to yourself, this is the year I begin but you don't and by the middle of the year you get upset and frustrated. Listen, firstly, a dream doesn't have to begin at the start of the year, we celebrate January as the first month of the year, but we determine the start of our dreams. So finally you decide to start taking small steps towards your dream, you enrol for a class to learn your new skill, celebrate your enrolment, and when you start attending, celebrate, because these small steps will definitely accumulate to make a giant leap, so it is only fair that you celebrate your small successes.

Forget the mistakes and regrets of yesterday,
Enjoy today and
Plan to have a great tomorrow,

"WE DETERMINE THE TIME WE START LIVING OUR DREAMS, SO ENJOY THE 'SMALL' SUCCESSES TOO, LIFE IS COMPLICATED ENOUGH"

YOU HAVE LIMITLESS CAPABILITIES & INFINITE POTENTIALS

You are not helpless or feeble or an inferior being, there is greatness in you and it is about time you start recognising this truth and living it. This is a gift you have been blessed with, what you choose to do with it depends on you.

It is no wonder when you ask a child what they dream of being, they see an endless world of possibilities, but that world begins to shrink rapidly, shaped by other people's realities, perceptions, societal pressures and many undesirable factors, until the dream turns into a figment of imagination or fizzles out completely, but thank God for those who carry on and follow their dreams to fulfil their purpose, they make others believe that it is possible.

Man is designed intricately and complex and this is the reason why after decades, even centuries, new music is still being written, composed and sung, new books are still been written, art works are still being created, and yet no two piece of work are ever the same, unless made so intentionally.

If that is not infinite and unlimited resources, I don't know what is

The workings of your mind is beyond what you can imagine

John Muir says 'the power of imagination makes us infinite'

You have unlimited potential, capacity, capabilities, it is not limited by time, by space; by distance or anything we will see as a limitation.

An unknown author wrote "It's not who you are that holds you back, it's who you think you're not,"

> "THE SORCERY & CHARM OF IMAGINATION, AND THE POWER IT GIVES TO THE INDIVIDUAL TO TRANSFORM HIS WORLD INTO A NEW WORLD OF ORDER AND DELIGHT, MAKES IT ONE OF THE MOST TREASURED OF ALL HUMAN CAPACITIES – Frank Barron"

Who do you think you are? The answer to this question will determine if you will succeed in life or if you will be a failure, there are people who know who they are but are afraid to admit it to themselves, and there are those who know their seeming limitation but defy the norm anyway and defy any limitation.

THE POWER OF YOUR HAPPINESS

Discover your excitement and zazz for life, it is so easy to forget what makes you smile, even easier to lose yourself in challenges and let them rob you of your happiness and joy but know this, that doing what you love to do is what brings you joy and this is what makes you confident in life. When you are unsatisfied with your life, you become unhappy and this unhappiness robs you of the ability to live a confident life, so why would you want to be unhappy. Therefore, surround yourself with people and stuff that make you happy, participate in activities that make you happy and makes you feel confident, do note that most people are too busy with their lives to make you feel better about yours, so the power lies in your hands, and that is a great thing isn't it? You have the power to decide to be happy or miserable, it is up to you to decide how you react to a situation

Most folks are as happy as they make up their minds to be. - Abraham Lincoln

There is more to life than being miserable, there are those that complain about anything and everything, they are unhappy about their lives and blame every one and every situation about their unhappiness but what they fail to realise is that the decision is solely theirs, you get out of your life what you put in. You have every right to be happy, yes, life can be full of ups and downs but how you react to those times is up to you.

"Have the courage to live. Anyone can die."
Robert Cody

LET GO OF YOUR COMFORT ZONE & DISCOVER A WORLD OF POSSIBILITIES

You have unlimited power, resources, health, wealth, peace, inspiration, wisdom, ability and creative power. Begin to discover these capabilities in you today by going beyond your comfort zone and daring to do the 'impossible'.

"Deep within man dwells those slumbering powers; powers that would astonish him, that he never dreamed of possessing; forces that would revolutionize his life if aroused and put into action" – Orison Swett Marden

"The potential of the average person is like a huge ocean unsailed, a new continent unexplored, a world of possibilities waiting to be released and channelled toward some great good" -Brian Tracy

The reason why most people complain about their lives and are unsatisfied with their lives is that man was made to achieve, to accomplish and to utilize his unlimited self and when you are not doing this; you are unsatisfied with your life. Your desire to do more and be greater than you are, is normal and natural, a God given quality, so wouldn't it just be easier to dream, aim and achieve? After all, what have you got to lose, and even if you fail, you just keep trying.

"I quit being afraid when my first venture failed and the sky didn't fall down" – Allen H. Neuharth

"THERE IS SO MUCH MORE YOU CAN BE AND DO BUT YOU CAN'T DISCOVER THEM UNTIL YOU VENTURE INTO A WORLD OF POSSIBILITIES"

I laughed the first time I read this quote but it is a very wise quote
So live your life care free, only be mindful of the unlimited you, decide to be happy, dream to influence your world, for that is when you will find fulfilment.

You were born to do remarkable things, so don't live your life like one who has no choice, live your life free, be enthusiastic and break beyond the bounds of limitations.

PLAY THE HAND YOU HAVE BEEN DEALT & BE GREAT AT IT

"Just because Fate doesn't deal you the right cards, it doesn't mean you should give up. It just means you have to play the cards you get to their maximum potential." - Les Brown

Life is no respecter of persons, it doesn't favour one person and despise the other, every person has this gift called life and what you chose to do with it is up to you, it does not matter the circumstances you are thrown into, okay, some people 'seem' to have it better than others, these are just conditions.

There are some very interesting definitions of 'condition', one says it is a state of being of a person; another says it is an existing state and the one that is really striking says 'it is a situation with respect to circumstances'.

So it is safe to say that conditions are not permanent, they are variables and they depend on something, conditions is a 'state' that depends on something or a circumstance.

An example is this, a person is born into a wealthy family, therefore your 'state of being' is wealthy and this depends on the fact that you are born into a certain circumstance.

Another person has a million pounds in the bank, your 'state of being' will be wealthy, say his circumstance changes, he loses all his money in a bad investment, his condition changes and his 'state' changes, so you see that conditions are not permanent, there are too many variables in this world for conditions to remain permanent.

"I don't believe in circumstances. The people who get on in this world are the people who get up and look for the circumstances they want, and, if they can't find them, make them. – G.B. Shaw, Mrs. Warren's Profession, 1893

LIFE IS SHORT, STRIKE THAT...LIFE IS FAST

Here is another lesson I have learnt, it has always been said that life is short, so do all you need to and make sure you make the most of your life, but taking it further, I have come to learn that not only is life short, it is fast and very fast indeed.

You cannot afford the luxury of procrastination or waiting to start your life. This is it right now; your life has begun, for some, it has gone farther than for others. But wherever you are, this is your life and it is moving fast. Remember that day you made up your mind to start on your dream, or that day you decided to start pursuing what you love doing, that day you said you were going to write that book or apply for your dream job or start up your business? Well, hey, it's 5 years already (or more) and you are still complaining about your life and still making plans to begin what you want.

Life is fast and the truth is that, if you live it or not, it will continue anyway, so why not stop procrastinating, you don't want to wake up one morning and wonder where the years went, start where you are today with what you have and LIVE!

IMPOSSIBLE THINGS TAKE A LITTLE LONGER

"Difficult things take a long time, impossible things a little longer". – André A. Jackson

It is easy to get lost in and be overwhelmed by situations we face, but you have to determine what you really want out of life and insist on achieving them, someone once said that life is a daring adventure, or a series of insane dares. Do you ever look at people who are achieving their desires, some may even be living the life you dream of, know that it is not impossible for you to be and live the life you want, the difference between the man who is successful and the one that is not, is in persistence and time.

"Look at a stone cutter hammering away at his rock, perhaps a hundred times without as much as a crack showing in it. Yet at the hundred-and-first blow it will split in two, and I know it was not the last blow that did it, but all that had gone before". - Jacob A. Riis

You may be doing all you know to do right now, it may be frustrating and discouraging not seeing any results, but don't despair or get flustered, just keep at what you are doing, your persistence will insist its way through and you will soon see the results you desire.
When you have done all you can, continuing on is that extra oomph that you require

"Success seems to be largely a matter of hanging on after others have let go". - William Feather

"Don't let the fear of the time it will take to accomplish something stand in the way of your doing it. The time will pass anyway; we might just as well put that passing time to the best possible use". – Earl Nightingale

YOUR DREAMS, THE POWER OF YOU

"Dream and give yourself permission to envision a You that you choose to be" – Joy Page

"Never laugh at anyone's dreams. People who don't have dreams don't have much." - Unknown

You wonder why we talk about dreams so much? It is because every person has a dream, it is inbuilt in a human being to imagine himself more than he is right now, to imagine being more and doing more.
In every being are talents waiting to be discovered, songs to be sung, books to be written, art to be painted, business to be started, dreams to be fulfilled.
Too many people are too comfortable being where they are, without even thinking they could be more and achieve more, they would rather remain with the familiar than reach out for the impossible.

Make up your mind to pursue those dreams and desires with a conviction that it is possible, don't let situations and circumstances tell you otherwise, don't let others discourage you, because they are too fearful to pursue their dreams, don't let the world system and status quo determine how far you go with your dreams

"If you can imagine it, you can achieve it. If you can dream it, you can become it - William Arthur ward"

"YOUR DREAMS MAKE YOU THE WEALTHIEST PERSON & BIGGEST INVESTMENT ON THIS EARTH, DON'T BE A MISSED OPPORTUNITY"

You might ask, what if I don't know what my dreams are, well think about what you are passionate about, what does your mind wander to when you are 'day dreaming', what do you think about that excites you and gets your heart racing? What if someone told you right now that you can do whatever, be whoever or go wherever you want to, without any limitations or anything to worry about, what would your thoughts be? Those are your dreams.

So if you have a dream today, blessed are you, because you are the wealthiest person on this earth. You are the greatest investment on earth because in you are potentials and talents waiting to be discovered and developed.

ALL THE WORLD'S A STAGE

These are some of the most powerful words ever written 'All the World's a stage' by Shakespeare. Yes, you have arrived, you are on your own time now, the world is your canvas, you are calling the shots, now what are you going to do about it?

Now the fun and adventure begins.

"Life is either a daring adventure or nothing" –Helen Keller

You have to dare to be you, you cannot fold your arms and do nothing for fear of failure, that will be cheating yourself and cheating others benefitting from what you can contribute to the world. Everything we see and have today is because someone had a dream and a vision, what if Albert Einstein did not dream, what if Beethoven did not have a dream, what if The great painters and authors did not have a dream, what if great pioneers of industries did not have a dream or a vision, what if Walt Disney did not have a dream, what would our world have been like today? Now think about what our tomorrow will look like if those with dreams refuse to pursue their dreams or lack the courage to, so do not cheat the world of what you have to give.

Quit being so afraid of everything; be bold, strong and courageous. The dreams you have, show you that it is possible, your mind dreams within the boundaries of possibilities, therefore, no matter how big the dream your mind conjures, know that it is possible and that is why your mind conjured it up in the first place, so it is up to you now, to begin to plan and take steps to making this dream a reality. Now be bold and have some fun, the world is waiting.

"QUIT BEING SO AFRAID OF EVERYTHING AND ANYTHING, GO HAVE SOME FUN & ADVENTURE, THE WORLD IS WAITING FOR YOU"

YOU DESERVE TO LIVE WITH EXCITEMENT & PASSION, SPICE IT UP

A lot of people have lost their passion for life, their excitement and enthusiasm, life has become a series of routine and they have lost their appeal for life. Things they used to get excited about now irritate them and they can go a whole day without finding a reason to smile or be happy. So how do you spice up your life and get back that excitement?

Find something you are passionate about, this works all the time, do something that makes you happy and that you like doing, and this takes the boring out of your life. When you are doing what you love, it helps build your confidence and self-esteem and rekindle your passion for waking up excited every morning.

Do something new, learn to be adventurous and discover new things, this depends on how daring you can be. Do something you have never done before that you've always wanted to do. It does not have to be something crazy, it can be trying a different cuisine, trying a food you have never had before or even making a different meal. Sometimes, we get stuck on the same meal routine every day; make something different that you haven't tried before.

Be creative, there are so many ways to spice up your life so look out for opportunities, think of what you can do right now, this week or this weekend, don't hesitate, procrastinate or put it off. You deserve to live an exciting life.

THE POWER OF FRIENDS

Don't underestimate the power of friendship and of friends, some people who are miserable always want to be alone, I always say that misery hates company and it is true. Of course it is great to learn to enjoy your own company, where you can be happy even if you are by yourself, that is great, but if that is not the case, then remember your good friends, those who are positive and are able to contribute to your happiness, not those who are critical and would even make you feel worse, suggest activities you can do with friends, go for a drink, or just visit with friends, sitting around in the house and having fun can be great fun too.

To have a friend and be a friend is what makes life worthwhile. – Unknown

"FRIENDS CAN BE A RAY OF SUNSHINE & BREATH OF FRESH AIR, SO CHOOSE WISELY, YOU DON'T HAVE TO BE FRIENDS WITH EVERYONE"

Having great friends with you make your life colorful, if you don't have a friend, then go out and make some friends, be a great friend to someone and make someone's day. Don't just make any friends, have friends that are doing well, who you admire, with who you can be your best.

"Pick your friends with care, they create the environment in which you will either thrive or wilt"

You become like those with whom you associate, so choose carefully.

SHOW UP FOR YOUR LIFE

Show up for your life and be present, this is your life and it is primarily up to you what you make of it, don't make anyone responsible for your life. This is your life, so pay great attention to it, be carefree but don't be careless with your life. Pay attention to making yourself happy because the responsibility of living the life you want lies solely on your shoulders, there are other factors that may contribute but the responsibility and decision is yours.

Don't get all boxed in and letting the wall close in on you, they tend to do that, so ive your life free, create the space to live largely and live well. Develop yourself, earn and do something new and don't let your thoughts limit you.

'Stop thinking in terms of limitations and start thinking in terms of possibilities"

Terry Josephson

Sometimes the biggest limits can come from our minds, the minds that have been conditioned by years of people saying no, or that you can't do some thing, the mind that has been conditioned by the negativity of others, and by the seeming impossibilities around us, how many times have you thought about doing something and immediately you dismiss it as impossible or your mind brings up excuses why it would not work, or how you previously tried and failed and instead of thinking of possibilities, you zero in on the reasons why it would not be possible, it is always easier to think of difficulties instead of opportunities.

LIVE OUT EXTRAORDINARILY

"Impossible is just a big word thrown around by small men who find it easier to live in the world they've been given than to explore the power they have to change it. Impossible is not a fact. It's an opinion. Impossible is not a declaration. It's a dare. Impossible is potential. Impossible is temporary. Impossible is nothing." —
Muhammad Ali

This is a very popular quote and it has inspired ordinary people to go ahead to do extraordinary things and I hope it does the same for you too because life is about taking risks and having the determination to forge ahead no matter what life throws your way.

One of the greatest things is to take your ordinary life and live it in an extra ordinary way, You don't want to live your life in fear or in quitting, it is always better to try and fail than not to try at all.

"To live is the rarest thing in the world. Most people exist, that is all." — Oscar Wilde

"LIFE IS NOT REALLY WORTH LIVING IF IT ISN'T LIVED EXTRAORDINARILY, THE WORLD HAS ENOUGH ORDINARY IN IT"

Never forget that life is a gift and you deserve to have a great one and that will not happen if you fold your arms and do nothing, it seems life will throw you difficult situations and challenges just to determine how badly you want it. Yes, you may see yourself as ordinary, but remember that there are 'ordinary' people who have gone on to do extraordinary things and you can do.

THE YOU'NIQUE CONSTANCY – FIND YOUR ZAZZ & OWN IT

Zazz: a quantifiable amount of something special, the essence of extreme coolness, the highest level of Flyness that one can possess - urban dictionary

That special thing that makes you, you
And yes, you are awesome and special but you have to believe it yourself. No two finger prints are ever the same, that says a lot about how unique you are so don't try living some one else's life, or equally bad, the life that someone else has mapped out for you.

It is not complicated, don't try to analyse it or over think it, you are awesome and great, much more than you think, so live like it and be who you really are. What do you see when you look in the mirror, what do you think about when you think of you? These are some of the questions that determine the way you see yourself and ultimately the way you decide to live your life.

So decide to live your life in the highest level and start working towards doing that, you deserve an opportunity to live a great and satisfying life and these opportunities abound, remember it all begins with you making a decision. So discover your zazz and live your life with style and class.

THE AMAZING YOU EFFECT: YOU'VE GOT STYLE & YOU'VE GOT CLASS

"Class is an aura of confidence that is being sure without being cocky. Class has nothing to do with money. Class never runs scared. It is self-discipline and self-

knowledge. It's the sure-footedness that comes with having proved you can meet life. "— Ann Landers

Class is the way in which you carry and present yourself, your overall confidence and demeanour.
Believe in yourself, believe in your ability to be who you want to be and do what you want to do, dress the part and act the part and walk the part. Walk with your head held high and your shoulders upright, you have nothing to be ashamed of, you have everything to be confident about.
Don't go through life like a nobody, don't talk and act like a nobody, you deserve to be noticed and you deserve to be admired, respected and loved, not just because of how you look or your outward appearance but also because of who you are.

"I wept when I saw a man without shoes, until I saw a man without class" - Les Brown

Be your biggest fan, love who you are and be your best, don't let people put you down or rob you of your self esteem, money is great but it doesn't buy you self esteem, you create your self esteem from who you are and what you think of you

CHAMPAGNE TASTE AND LEMONADE POCKET?

Don't be afraid of expensive things, nothing is too good for you. If you have had a cheap mind set for a long time, then it is time to change your thoughts and perception. Get comfortable around expensive things and expensive people. Wealth is a way of thinking and not a dollar amount in the bank. Your wealth begins with your mind, when you see something as too expensive for you; your mind immediately shuts off the possibilities of you getting it.
Hey, if you have never bought a pair of shoes for $1,000, go to the shop and try them on, this will begin to reset your mind and how you think about money.

'Money is just a point of view, how can you be rich if you think $200,000 is a lot of money?" – Rich Dad Guide to Investing

"Never use the word "cheap". Today everybody can look chic in inexpensive clothes (the rich buy them too). There is good clothing design on every level today. You can be the chicest thing in the world in a T-shirt and jeans — it's up to you."

— Karl Lagerfeld

Don't plan to enjoy your life 'someday', that day is today, so start from where you are and begin to enjoy your life. Don't put off the start of your life to sometime in the future, don't dream of 'starting' a great life some time, live your great life and your dreams, now.

Les Brown once said you cannot shrink into greatness, you can only expand into greatness, so what? Are you going to downsize and minimize or are you going to expand your means? The decision is yours to make, you can have an expensive pocket for your expensive taste.

YOU CAN'T SOAR WITH HEAVY SUITCASES

"There are no constraints on the human mind, no walls around the human spirit, no barriers to our progress except those we ourselves erect – Ronald Reagan

You can be your best friend or easily become your worst enemy, don't criticise yourself or be too hard on yourself, let your heart and mind dwell on pleasant thoughts that will free you from the heavy burden and allow you to fly.

Have you met some people who are constantly tired? No matter how much they rest and sleep, they are still tired, one of the reasons why is what their minds are dwelling on, you can lay on your bed and let your mind wander through all the awful thoughts, when you rise up, you will realise that you are so tired, true, you haven't gone anywhere or done any demanding activities, but your mind has and it will tell on your body.

When you have thoughts of success, and your mind dwells on great and happy thoughts, you will find you have strength, your life will begin to flourish and it will influence everything and everyone around you

Let me tell you another secret, you have done some incredible things in your life, so when you find yourself feeling down, doubting yourself and not feeling right, remind yourself of remarkable things you have done in the past, of little triumphs and victories you have won in the past, if you do not do this, no one else will. Drop the suitcases of regret, pain, hurt and the past and spread your wings and fly.

REDEFINE YOUR BELIEF SYSTEM

Many of us often have the belief that we are not good enough, that is just one of many destroying beliefs that takes a hold of our minds, we often process these thoughts many times a day. When you see someone else who has what you don't have, do you think that you are not going to have it, or you are not going to have the success that they have?

Start redefining your thoughts and beliefs, what if for today, you choose to believe that you good enough to be and have what you want, you choose to believe that you are strong enough, wise enough, good looking enough, kind enough, what if for today, you choose to believe that you are doing well in your life?

Your belief system is one of the most important things you have to develop, don't just believe anything about yourself, your belief system is what determines how far you will go in achieving and living a good life. Your life is as you choose to see it; your life is a reflection of what you believe, so focus on the right beliefs.

LIFE IS A BEAUTIFUL THING

"There are only two ways to live your life, one is as though nothing is a miracle, the other is as though everything is a miracle" - Albert Einstein

"Life is full of beauty, notice it, notice the bumble bee, the small child and the smiling faces, smell the rain and feel the wind, live your life to the fullest potential and fight for your dreams" - Ashley Smith

You are the captain of your life and master of your fate, so love and laugh your way through life.

Life comes with challenges, that is no secret, but it also comes with beauty and marvel so which do you choose to see? It is your choice how you live life and what you do with it, if you don't do anything, you are going to be miserable anyway, so why don't you make an effort to uplift you and enjoy this beautiful thing called life.

Don't live your life based on your bad experiences and forget to see the good experiences in life, don't allow these bad experiences dictate the rest of your life. Everyday is a new opportunity given to us to live life to the full, today is the beginning of the rest of your life, the sun rises every morning to remind you to grab a new opportunity to live a great life.

BE A DISCOVERER & EXPLORER

"Be a Columbus to whole new continents and worlds within you, opening new channels, not of trade but of thought" – Henry David Thoreau

There is more to you than even you can fathom, so why don't you spend the time discovering who you are and taking pleasure in doing just that.

Invest in yourself and invest in others,

"To dream anything that you want to dream, that's the beauty of the human mind, to do anything that you want to do, that's the strength of the human will, to trust yourself to test your limits, that's the courage to succeed" – Bernard Edmonds

You are the richest person and wisest investment on the face of the planet, because in you are songs yet unsung, books yet unwritten, movies yet unmade, stories yet untold, words yet unspoken, dreams yet unfulfilled, talents yet undiscovered, ideas yet unachieved.

So you have a lifetime to discover these about yourself, so why not start today, focus and spend your energy on discovering the great things about yourself and celebrating them, you have a lifetime ahead of you.

FORGET THE EXPECTATIONS

Our lives are always full of activities and busyness, we are surrounded with people in every area of our lives and these people have different expectations of us, so we are forced to be different things to different people to meet their expectations of us, this is so exhausting. It is easy to go on like this for years until you lose yourself in other's expectations, and not also forgetting our own expectations of ourselves too.

Everyday, we plan to meet the expectations of our colleagues, our boss, our customers, our parents, our children, our friends, our selves and sometimes, even expectations of strangers. Yes, be a good person; be great at your work and business, be a wonderful partner and parent etc., but the point is not meeting all these expectations at the cost of losing ourselves. Don't define yourself by other people's expectations of you.

Take the time out today to just forget what others expect of you, forget what you expect of you and just savour who you are and enjoy it, at this very moment.

YOU WERE BORN AN ORIGINAL, DON'T DIE A COPY

To be original means to be the source from which a copy, reproduction, or translation is made. Not copied, imitated, or translated; new; fresh and genuine.

"If you want to be original just try being yourself, because God has never made two people exactly alike." – Bernard Meltzer

"To be yourself in a world that is constantly trying to make you something else is the greatest accomplishment."- Ralph Waldo Emerson

Do not underestimate the power of your originality, many people would rather be like, act like and look like someone else rather than themselves that is dying a copy. To be your best self is the most powerful tool you have, no two people are the same and there is a reason for that, everyone is unique and contributes to life in a unique way, celebrate your uniqueness and originality.

OVERCOME YOUR FEARS

"Inaction breeds doubt and fear. Action breeds confidence and courage. If you want to conquer fear, do not sit home and think about it. Go out and get busy." – Dale Carnegie

"Waiting to develop courage is just another form of procrastination. The most successful people take action while they're afraid!" – Unknown

Remember the last time you wanted to do something but didn't? Or hesitated? Fear is that voice that stopped you and made you doubt yourself. **Fear is the voice that tells us, if we try, the probability of failure will be higher than that of success and then we do nothing instead.**

The good news is that everyone feels fear, and the better news is that you can certainly feel the fear and do it anyway. One of the best ways to overcome your fear is to take action.

DEFINE YOUR STRENGTH

What you think about yourself matters a great deal. The thoughts you think and the words you speak to you, do they stir up strength in you or do they make you lose confidence in the strength you have? Strength is the ability to see, believe in and use a greater force, and this force is a weapon in your hand, which helps you overcome in any and every situation, it is not just enough to have this strength in you, you have to use it, to win in any hopeless situation, and constant wielding of this force, makes you big, irrespective of your physical stature and that, my friend is what matters most.

'There are two primary choices in life: to accept conditions as they exist, or accept the responsibility for changing them' - Denis Waitley

It is the person of strength who perseveres and continues even when it seems nothing is going right, be sure that with this strength, comes determination, with the determination, comes courage, with courage comes perseverance, and with this perseverance, comes triumph and success. A brave man is not one who does not have fear, but one who can do the right thing and forges ahead in the face of fear, the one good thing about fear is that it teaches us who we are. Without fear, we wouldn't know what we are made of; you have to find courage in your strength.

" YOU ARE BRAVER THAN YOU CAN IMAGINE & STRONGER THAN EVEN YOU WOULD BELIEVE, THE FUN IS IN MEETING LIFE HEAD ON AND WINNING"

The strength and resolve you have in you, your stubborn faith, can wear down any trouble or challenge, it may take a while but remember that you are designed to always be the last man standing, so don't you dare give up because you are more stubborn than anything that you may face.

GO ON, BE FAB!

To me, Fabulousness means that:

1. I can enjoy my life, smile and laugh and be carefree. Knowing that I deserve the best.

2. It is great to enjoy a treat, now and again. I love the chocolate cakes

3. That I am unique and gorgeous, and I celebrate my uniqueness and I am confident in this.

4. There is a lot to discover about me, so I would not waste the time listening or

thinking about other people's negative opinions about me, I am having a great time discovering how great I am and loving it.

5. My thoughts, perceptions and inner being affect my outward appearance and aura; I see the world the way I think, so when I'm happy, the world is happy.

6. Life is bigger than I can think; I can be who and what I want to be. I can live loudly, largely and with gusto everyday.

10. I am simply and marvelously FABULOUS!

BE AUTHENTIC

To be authentic means you are true, you are genuine, the real thing, and with nothing bogus or fake

There is nothing more beautiful than seeing a person being themselves. Imagine going through your day being unapologetically you." – Steve Maraboli

This is one of the most important truths you should believe and the most important habit to form, and that is to be the best you and be authentic. Society is constantly telling you who you should be and what you should be and what you ought to be, and if you are anything otherwise, it makes you feel guilty or ashamed. The world will be a much happier place if people are happy with their best selves, if they can be what they want to be and not have to conform to what others think.

Don't ever be ashamed of the person you are or that body that you have. Why would you be? You're fabulous just the way you are! Rock what your mamma gave you and embrace who you are. It is more fun discovering who you are, your talents, skills, strengths, personality even the quirks and experimenting with your discoveries.

"WHY WOULD I WANT TO BE A POOR IMITATION OF SOMEONE ELSE, THIS IS PURELY EXHAUSTING, I CAN BE THE BEST OF ME AND THIS IS MORE EXCITING"

When you are authentic, then you will have more confidence and have more energy, to be someone else is just exhausting, Love yourself, respect yourself, and celebrate you.

To be nobody but yourself in a world which is doing its best, night and day, to make you everybody else means to fight the hardest battle which any human being can fight; and never stop fighting – E.E Cummings

GIVE YOURSELF PERMISSION

Give yourself permission to live and to enjoy your life, some people are afraid to enjoy what they have, either because they feel they don't deserve it or because they believe they will lose it. Don't go around thinking about that, don't fill your mind with thoughts of lack and shortage.
The only person who can give you the permission to have a great life is staring back at you in the mirror.
Some people beat themselves up over the smallest things and mistakes, for example, if you cheat on a diet, your whole day is ruined and you feel like a loser, stop such thoughts, so what you cheated on your diet, let it go and continue on the diet, life is too short to live like this.

Give yourself permission to make some mistakes, you are not perfect, you are human, you make mistakes and learn from them and become a better person. Don't be too hard on yourself if you don't meet the goals you have set for yourself. Don't call yourself an idiot because you made a mistake, or think yourself a failure because you failed in achieving a project, you are so much more than your actions so don't let them define you.

Life is too short to live in such a limiting manner.

BELIEVE IT OR NOT, THESE WORDS DESCRIBE YOU

"The way you treat yourself sets the standard for others." – Sonya Friedman

SUAVE – The ultimate way to say something or someone is the coolest there is. Someone who is suave is so radically cool, that the words cool, swell, sweet or chill can't even begin to apply; it means they are charming, confident, pleasant in manner and elegant.

FIERCE – A word that can describe something as outstanding, really cool, eye catching and of exceptional quality. It is also used to describe when somebody is looking fly or really good. Someone who can say, "This is not how we do it, this is how I do it"

FABULOUS – Extremely pleasing and unbelievably incredible, this is used to describe someone who believes the best of themselves and is not afraid to show it. Someone who expects the world to treat them as incredible

SEXY –"Sex appeal is fifty percent what you've got and fifty percent what people think you've got." – Sophia Loren.
So, sexy is half determined by what you look like, and more by who you are and how you carry yourself. Sexy also describes a person who is able to make what they have and what they don't have, work for them.

PRACTICE COMPASSION FOR OTHERS

Compassion teaches us not to focus solely on our problems and ourselves; it helps us look beyond our selves to someone else.

Compassion involves your willingness to place yourself in someone else's shoes, to focus on someone else and imagine what it is like to be in their predicament. If someone reacts or responds to you in a negative manner, don't react immediately, try and imagine their predicament and place yourself in their shoes, and try to understand where they are coming from. Often times, you might find out that the person has had a really bad day or is having an awful week. Many times, people's negative actions are reactions to the frustrations and pains that they are feeling, compassion helps you empathise and understand that other people's problems and frustrations are every bit as real as and sometimes, far worse, than our own.

So develop and practice compassion and when you take the attention off yourself and the little things 'ruining your life', you will be surprised to find you have a lot to be grateful for.

YOU ARE AS AMAZING AS YOU LET YOURSELF BE

You are as amazing as you let yourself be. Let me repeat that. You are as amazing as you let yourself be. – Elizabeth Alraune

You are wonderful. Valuable. Worthwhile. Lovable. Not because others think so. Self worth comes from only one place: self. – Karen Salmansohn

So quit looking at you as ordinary, a man's mind cannot be fathomed, and the abilities, capabilities and capacity of his spirit cannot even be explained in human terms, so the next time you look at yourself in the mirror and don't like what you see, think about these things, if you don't call you amazing, remarkable, wonderful, beautiful, no one else will.

You can be your best friend or easily become your worst enemy, don't criticize yourself, don't be too hard on yourself, be constantly reminded that you are as amazing as you let yourself be.

"Having a low opinion of yourself is not "modesty". It's self-destruction. Holding your uniqueness in high regard is not "egotism". It's a necessary precondition to happiness and success." – Bobbe Sommer

Whatever you are doing, love yourself for doing it. Whatever you are feeling, love yourself for feeling it. – Thaddeus Golas

YOU ARE ALL KIND OF WONDERFUL

You see, life is a gift and it is a precious gift so do not waste it, situations come just to distract you from enjoying this precious gift but you have to decide to enjoy your life, this is a decision only you can make and you better make it quickly. And way to do this is to acknowledge and know that you are All Kinds Of Wonderful!!!

Don't let anything or anyone take your power away from you, the power you have to respond to situations the way you ought to, 'Life is 10% of what happens to you and 90% of how you react to it'.

Love yourself, it does not matter what you think you look like and what you may perceive as your faults, remember, they are just perceptions, there are many times when we find out that what we may dislike about ourselves are what others love about us, a popular saying is that beauty is in the eye of the beholder, look at yourself in the mirror and love what you see, when God made you, he made you perfect and wonderful, he did not forget to add or remove something in the creation process.

OWN YOUR POWER

To dream anything that you want to dream, that's the beauty of the human mind, to do anything that you want to do, that's the strength of the human will, to trust yourself to test your limits, that's the courage to succeed – Bernard Edmonds

You have done some incredible things in your life, so when you find yourself feeling down, doubting yourself and not feeling right, remind yourself of remarkable things you have done in the past, of little triumphs and victories you have won.

There are no constraints on the human mind, no walls around the human spirit, no barriers to our progress except those we ourselves erect – Ronald Reagan

Think on those things that seemed to be a huge problem at one time or the other in your life, and you thought you were never going to make it through that challenge, but you are still here today and may even have forgotten about the challenges. Listen, you have done some incredible things in your life, when you find yourself feeling down, doubting yourself and not feeling right, remind yourself of remarkable things you have done in the past, of little triumphs and victories you have won in the past.

SHOW YOUR TRUE COLOURS

One of the best ways to feel better about you is to dress real good, when you feel down and lethargic, that is the best time to bring out your best, look your best and smell good. We are often tempted to dress according to our moods, if you are in a good mood; you wear something bright and vice versa.

Nothing boosts your energy like a splash of confidence and this confidence always comes from looking great and feeling good about yourself.

Colors give beauty to things and make them vibrant and full of life, colors attract even more positive energy. Don't blend into the background, dull colors make life boring and dreary and sour your mood, so it doesn't matter the season or weather, adding that splash of color will brighten up your day.
Look good, wear great colors and walk with your head held high because you are worthy of being noticed.

CHOOSE THE FREEDOM LIFESTYLE

What is freedom? It is not a destination it is a lifestyle. The freedom lifestyle is choosing your ideal life and living that way with no restrictions. This is often tied to entrepreneurs but it also applies to you too. The freedom lifestyle is making more money smartly, having more time off and living the life that you love, having a fully rounded and rich life that you have designed. This freedom is available to everyone; you just need the courage to choose it.

"You are not born a winner. You are not born a loser. You are born a chooser" - anonymous

Firstly, irrespective of where you are in your life right now, you must believe that it is possible to design the life you want and to achieve it. Then you must make the choice to achieve your goal and be determined and disciplined enough to go after it. The only way to failure is quitting so decide not to give up, even when you face seemingly insurmountable challenges. Plan the lifestyle you want and then plan how to use the resources you have now to achieve that lifestyle. It's in the choices and the planning and determination.

LIVE INTENTIONALLY

Living intentionally means to be conscious of the choices you make in your life. Every one has a plan for their life (Well, if you don't, then I suggest you start making one immediately), and these plans are set in motion by the choices you make and activities you make your priority.

We are humans and we make choices every day, your life today is as a result of choices you made yesterday, every choice you make every single day is either taking you towards your goals or away from them. It is therefore very important to be conscious of the decisions you make; this is what it means to live on purpose.

You can live your life consciously, determining in advance the outcomes you want to experience. You are already doing this in your life anyway, from when you wake up till when you go to sleep, you are making choices and decision. You just have to become more aware and conscious of your decisions and priorities.

For example, you plan to write a book and become a best selling author, what you choose to do every day will either take you towards this goal or away from it, instead of sitting down to write a few words, do you decide to watch TV instead or spend another 2 hours on Facebook. The little choices you make all sums up to making your life. However, if you are into social media marketing, then spending that 2 hours on Facebook is the best choice for you.

Decide what is important to you and make conscious choices towards your goals.

LIFE IS NOT SET IN STONE

Some time ago, someone sent me an article, which I believe is perfect to illustrate this point, I don't know the author so apologies for not giving credit, it goes:

Over time, I've discovered there is no finish line or absolutes for everyone in life, our tracks are different and our durations are different. The only thing we have in common is the same empire. For instance, someone graduates at the age of 20 and struggles for another 5 years to get a job; another might graduate at 25 and get a job immediately. A fellow becomes a Director at 38 and dies at 56, another becomes a Director at 55 and lives to be 90. One person makes his fortune at 30 but loses it all at 40, another struggles financially all his life then makes his fortune at 40 and enjoys it, you get where I am going with this right? Life is full of twists, turn ups and downs, and many more surprises and disappointment.

Life offers each and every one of us different opportunities, it is up to each one of us to patiently prepare, wait, recognise and utilise every opportunity. We learn on the way, no one has it all or knows it all.

Life is a process and not a destination, not everyone gets the same start in life, so get rid of the thought that life is set in stone. The truth is that it is a process, where you are today can change tomorrow; it is all up to you.

CONFIDENCE, THE NEW SEXY

Self-confidence is the certainty you have that comes from believing in yourself, an assurance that comes from knowing that you are unique and special.

"It is safe to say that confidence comes from the real you, knowing, liking you and being happy with you. To be beautiful means to be yourself. You don't need to be accepted by others. You need to accept yourself." – Thich Nhat Hanh

Self confidence shows in your countenance and in your attitude, do note that self confidence is not pride, it is the humility that comes from a person who knows they have the option to be proud but choose humility instead. It is an attractive force field around you that attracts others to you, while pride is a barrier that repels them. Confidence does not need much talking as it shows in the way you carry yourself, your perception, your attitude and the way you relate with people and respond to life generally. The person who argues that they have confidence most likely does not.

Confidence is one of the attributes that attract others to you, it is indeed a strong attractive quality, it is being happy with you and it reflects in your smile and the warmth you carry with you that makes others want to be a part of your life.

GO ON, LIVE, LOVE & LAUGH

The world can be a dreary and bleak place, you only have to listen to the news to hear the worst of it all, but the great news is that you can always make your own world, this doesn't mean hiding your head in the sand and being unaware of what is going on around you, it means, knowing and acknowledging what is going on around you but still creating your own atmosphere and not letting the circumstances around you determine how you live your life or who you are. There are people who are like trees in the wind, they sway wherever the wind goes, but there are others who stand firm and refuse to be moved no matter how strong the wind howls and batters.

Here is a pretty interesting lesson I have learnt and it is that, I can love, laugh and live, I can enjoy life and not be apologetic about deciding to live a life I love, I don't have to join the millions out there who complain about their lives, I can live a satisfying life, be who I want to be, go where I want to go and do things I love and I don't need to apologise to anyone for these choices.
When you love, love fully, without restraint or holding back
When you live, live largely, energetically and with gusto, without regret or apology
When you laugh, laugh often, wholly, with life, and wholeheartedly, without fear.

STOP WORRYING SO MUCH

Control your own destiny or someone else will – Jack Welch

Many people have made worry a part of their lives, they cannot go a day without worrying, some believe by worrying that they are being responsible, however, worrying is just a bad habit that has negative effect on your entire being. You have more control over your life than you think and let's face it, no one else can really do a better job of your life than you can so quit worrying.

Worrying is imagining a worse case scenario; it is imagining and anticipating things that COULD happen, making things appear worse than they actually are. If you allow it, your mind would run wild and conjure up events that aren't even remotely likely.

Worry steals your joy and keeps you occupied from thinking about a solution, it is a negative habit that makes you use your imagination to create things you don't want. It is better to be exhausted from effort than to be tired of doing nothing but worrying.

So stop worrying so much and instead apply your energy to thinking about solutions to the things you want to worry about.

The bottom line is that it is your choice to get rid of the negativity and worry and focus on the solutions and hopes.

BROADEN YOUR LIFE

In the end, it's not going to matter how many breaths you took, but how many moments took your breath away – Shing xiong

Life is so much more than routine, life is bigger than you can fathom and much more diverse and more colorful than you can imagine and all these are for your enjoyment, they are for you to experience and enjoy. You may say that you like your routine and would not like anything outside of it but how would you know you would enjoy it or not if you don't try it first.

Different experiences broaden and enrich your life, it makes it well rounded and makes you more interesting, to yourself and to others. People would love to have a conversation with you because you have a broad range of topics and subject to talk about. Remember that your experiences are what matter, creating great memories that make you smile.

Change is good, even if you are not comfortable with it, it is easier to stay in our comfort zone, but be adventurous with your life and be more daring, try different things, make new friends, even something as simple as taking a different route to work, or going some place you have never been before. Gain new experiences by trying something different or doing things a different way, This world is vast and life is full of so many experiences and it is all made for you to enjoy, be bold and daring and choose to enjoy a well-rounded, robust and rich life.

LIVE OUT LOUD

Don't be boring, there is so much of life to experience, at least with the experience comes an ability to make an informed opinion. Some people are so boring that their conversations have been the same for years and this is because their conversations consist of the same experiences that's based on their limited life. Don't let people become accustomed to or worse, be able to predict your conversation.

A few years ago, I got so bored, my life had fallen into a routine, And I realized that even the music on my iPhone had remained the same for months and I was listening to the same music over and over again and I thought, how boring can you be, even the Apps on my device had been there for a long time, I made a decision that day and I changed all the music and Apps on my iPhone and my other devices, and have been doing that often.

Rediscover your passion for life and keep the excitement alive, Get involved in activities that will infuse the excitement into your life.

DO SOMETHING NICE FOR SOMEONE ELSE/GIVE BACK

We talked about compassion and putting yourself in someone else's shoes, this is a great way of taking the focus off yourself; it is also a great way to appreciate what you have. Take a step forward and do something nice for someone else, there is joy that cannot be explained when you give back. Something as little as a smile or a hello to a stranger can totally make their day.

Be willing to help others and be nice to them, sometimes some people do not appreciate it or may even be rude to you, but keep up with it, you are doing it for your sake.

A Quick Note From Angel

Thank you to everyone who has bought and read this book, I hope it has reminded you to take action for the life you want, it is great to connect with you, please check out my other books, I hope you have even more fun with them. Please drop me a line to tell me what you think and I would kindly ask you not to redistribute or share this eBook without my permission.

Printed in Great Britain
by Amazon